THE *Massachusetts* COLONY

Our Thirteen Colonies

SPIRIT
of America®

THE *Massachusetts* COLONY

By Barbara A. Somervill

Content Adviser: Marla Miller, Ph.D., Director, Public History Program,
University of Massachusetts, Amherst, Massachusetts

The
Child's
World®

The Child's World®
Chanhassen, Minnesota

6

THE *Massachusetts* COLONY

Published in the United States of America by The Child's World®
PO Box 326 • Chanhassen, MN 55317-0326 • 800-599-READ • www.childsworld.com

Acknowledgments
The Child's World®: Mary Berendes, Publishing Director

Editorial Directions, Inc.: E. Russell Primm, Editorial Director; Melissa McDaniel, Line Editor; Elizabeth K. Martin, Assistant Editor; Olivia Nellums, Editorial Assistant; Susan Hindman, Copy Editor; Joanne Mattern, Proofreader; Kevin Cunningham, Peter Garnham, Ruthanne Swiatkowski, Fact Checkers; Tim Griffin/IndexServ, Indexer; Cian Loughlin O'Day, Photo Researcher; Linda S. Koutris, Photo Selector

Photo
Cover: Francis G. Mayer/Corbis; Art Resource, NY: 14; Bettmann/Corbis: 15, 19, 21, 34; Corbis: 9 (The Mariner's Museum), 12, 18. Getty Images/Hulton Archive: 17, 27, 28, 31, 35; Library of Congress, Washington, D.C.: 24; North Wind Picture Archives: 6, 8, 10, 11, 16, 20, 22, 25, 30; Stock Montage: 13, 23, 29, 32.

Library of Congress Cataloging-in-Publication Data
Somervill, Barbara A.
  The Massachusetts Colony / by Barbara Somervill.
    p. cm.
  "Spirit of America."
  Summary: Traces the history of Massachusetts from 8000 B.C. when hunter-gatherer clans traveled there, through more than 150 years as a European colony, to 1788 when it became the sixth state in the Union. Includes bibliographical references and index.
  ISBN 1-56766-616-7 (lib. bdg. : alk. paper)
  1. Massachusetts—History—Colonial period, ca. 1600–1775—Juvenile literature. 2. Massachusetts—History—1775–1865—Juvenile literature. [1. Massachusetts—History—Colonial period, ca. 1600–1775. 2. Massachusetts—History—1775–1865.] I. Title.
  F67.S695 2003
  974.4—dc21   2002151353

15   20   28

Contents

Chapter ONE   *The People of the Dawn*   6

Chapter TWO   *Saints, Strangers, and Sachems* 12

Chapter THREE   *The Bay Colony*   18

Chapter FOUR   *The Shot Heard 'Round the World* 26

Chapter FIVE   *The Sixth State*   32

                  Time Line   36

                  Glossary Terms   37

                  *Massachusetts Colony's
                  Founding Fathers*   38

                  For Further Information   39

                  Index   40

Chapter ONE

The People of the Dawn

THE FIRST HUMANS TO LIVE IN WHAT IS NOW Massachusetts arrived about 10,000 years ago. They hunted huge elephant-like animals called mammoths and mastodons. They also gathered roots, berries, and nuts.

By 5000 B.C., the huge animals had died out. People began hunting smaller creatures such as deer, moose, bears, and raccoons. They also started growing squash, corn, beans, and pumpkins. These people lived in small villages.

Prehistoric Americans hunted large prey in groups to increase their chances of a successful hunt.

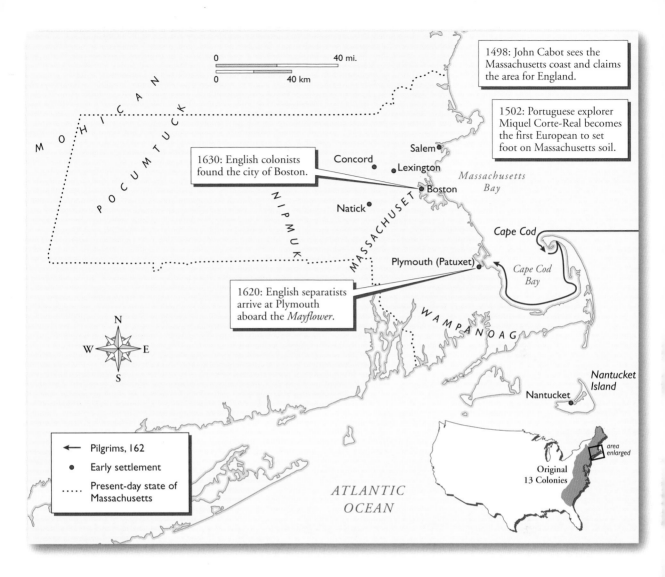

Within the map:

1498: John Cabot sees the Massachusetts coast and claims the area for England.

1502: Portuguese explorer Miquel Corte-Real becomes the first European to set foot on Massachusetts soil.

1630: English colonists found the city of Boston.

1620: English separatists arrive at Plymouth aboard the *Mayflower*.

MOHICAN

POCUMTUCK

NIPMUK

MASSACHUSET

WAMPANOAG

Salem
Concord
Lexington
Boston
Natick
Massachusetts Bay
Cape Cod
Cape Cod Bay
Plymouth (Patuxet)
Nantucket
Nantucket Island

ATLANTIC OCEAN

0   40 mi.
0   40 km

N W E S

Legend:
→ Pilgrims, 162
• Early settlement
···· Present-day state of Massachusetts

area enlarged
Original 13 Colonies

Between 2,000 and 3,000 years ago, new people swept into the area. They spoke the Algonquian language. Other groups living on the east coast of North America also spoke Algonquian. These groups traded with each other. Algonquian groups in Massachusetts included the Wampanoag, the Nipmuc, the Massachuset, and the Mohican.

Massachusetts Colony at the time of the first European settlement

7

▶ Mohican history and legend say that a great people came from the west and the north to finally settle in the east. Later, these people split into groups, one of which became the Mohicans.

The Massachuset lived in the area near what is now Boston. The Nipmuc settled in the central mountains. Mohican villages straddled the border between present-day Massachusetts and New York. The Wampanoag lived along the Massachusetts coast and on nearby islands, in the direction in which the sun rose. Their name, Wampanoag, means "people of the dawn." The Wampanoag's chief was called the grand sachem.

Early Native Americans used every part of the animals that they hunted.

8

The Native people in Massachusetts lived in seasonal villages. During the spring and summer, they lived in villages near their crop fields. After the harvest, the people moved into the forest, where the hunting was better. Their homes were called wigwams. These were wooden frames covered with grass or bark mats. At moving time, the people simply took the mats and left. The frames remained in place for when the people returned the next season.

A painting by John White, an artist from the 1500s, shows a tidy Native American village. The remarkable detail in the artist's work provided many clues about the way of life in such villages.

Everyone in the native villages helped out. Men hunted, fished, made tools and weapons, and protected the village. They built canoes from birch trees and traveled along water routes for trading. Women turned animal hides into clothes and shoes. They smoked or dried meat, fish, beans, and corn. Women also tilled fields and planted crops. Children picked nuts and berries and watered crops.

By A.D. 1600, about 40,000 native people lived in what is now Massachusetts. Roughly 12,000 were Wampanoag. At that time, Europeans began trading along the Massachusetts coast. Europeans brought cloth, weapons, glass—and disease.

Between 1614 and 1620, three major **epidemics** struck native people in Massachusetts. Because the Native Americans had never before come in contact with diseases such as smallpox, plague, or even measles, their bodies could not fight them. Ten Wampanoag villages were completely wiped out. Others lost a third or more of their members. Only 7,000 Wampanoag survived the epidemics. The Massachuset villages were also devastated. Never again would Native Americans in Massachusetts be as strong.

Many early Europeans hoped to make their fortune hunting, trapping, and trading with the Native Americans. Beaver and other furs brought enormous profit.

MASSASOIT, THE WAMPANOAG SACHEM WHO BEFRIENDED THE SETTLERS, DIED IN 1661. This ended years of peace between the English settlers and the Wampanoag. Massasoit's son Wamsutta (Alexander) became the new sachem. Wamsutta watched the English take over Wampanoag hunting grounds and farmland. He saw natives forced to follow Puritan laws and religion. English settlers showed no respect for Wampanoag beliefs.

The Puritans brought Wamsutta to Plymouth to answer questions about his people. Wamsutta became sick during questioning and headed home. He died on the way. Wamsutta's brother Metacom—whom the English called King Philip—became sachem. He thought the English had poisoned his brother. He also hated the Puritans because they continued to take over the Wampanoag lands. Metacom looked for any excuse to fight the settlers.

In 1675, Metacom's excuse arrived. A Christian native named John Sassamon was killed. The Puritans hanged three Wampanoag warriors for the crime. Metacom and his warriors attacked and burned several colonial villages.

King Philip's War lasted from 1675 to 1676. The Wampanoags joined with other groups, such as the Nipmuc and the Pocumtuck, to fight against the English and natives who were allied with them. Some native groups chose not to fight for either side. Fifty of 90 English villages were burned or damaged. Six hundred English and 3,000 natives died. Colonists sent 500 natives to Spain or the **West Indies** to be sold as slaves. Metacom's wife and son were among those sold. He said, "My heart breaks . . . I am ready to die."

In 1676, Metacom was shot through the heart and killed. The Puritans beheaded Metacom's body. They displayed the head on a pole for 25 years. King Philip's War was the worst fighting ever on Massachusetts's soil.

11

Chapter TWO

Saints, Strangers, and Sachems

King Henry VII gave John Cabot and his three sons permission to look for islands and foreign lands in the name of England.

THE FIRST EUROPEANS TO SAIL NEAR WHAT IS now Massachusetts were most likely Vikings, who came from Norway. In around the year 1000, Vikings arrived in Newfoundland, an island off the coast of Canada. They explored the coastline, possibly as far south as Massachusetts.

In 1498, John Cabot, an Italian sailing for the English, saw the Massachusetts coast. Though he did not go ashore, he claimed the land for England.

The first European to set foot on Massachusetts soil was Portuguese explorer Miguel Corte-Real in 1502. Corte-Real's ship sank, and his crew lived with Native Americans until 1511. Nearly 100 years went by before the English became interested in Massachusetts. In 1602, Bartholomew Gosnold sailed into Massachusetts waters.

He named the area Cape Cod because the waters were full of codfish.

Today, we call the first European settlers in Massachusetts **Pilgrims.** At the time, they were known as **Separatists.** The Separatists believed that the Church of England was too corrupt to be changed. They wanted to break away from it entirely. In the 1600s, English people who did not follow the Church of England were punished. The Separatists were among those who suffered for their religion.

The Separatists decided to build a colony in North America. They planned to sail in two ships, the *Mayflower* and the *Speedwell.* But the *Speedwell* leaked badly, so its passengers shifted to the *Mayflower.* On September 16, 1620,

In the 1600s, England refused to allow any religion except the Anglican Church, under penalty of death. Fearing for their lives, many Puritans sailed to North America in hopes of finding religious freedom.

Interesting Fact

▶ One meaning of *pilgrim* is a person who journeys to a foreign land. Not all the *Mayflower* Pilgrims were Separatists. Some simply went to America in hopes of escaping poverty.

The Pilgrims' landing at Plymouth Rock was an event that would shape the rest of American history.

102 people huddled together on the *Mayflower*. The ship was overcrowded with "saints" and "strangers." The Separatists called themselves saints. Soldiers and nonreligious people on the ship were called strangers.

The *Mayflower* sailed into a nightmare. Early winter storms tossed the ship about. Icy waves slapped the decks. The travelers were wet, cold, and hungry. When they weren't seasick, they ate hard biscuits, cold beans, and salt meat.

After 65 days at sea, the weary travelers caught sight of Massachusetts. They had planned to settle near Virginia, where there was already an English settlement. Tired and sick, they gladly chose Cape Cod instead. The group decided to build their town on the site of an abandoned Native American village. They named their town Plymouth, after the English port from which they sailed.

To maintain order, the Pilgrims wrote up laws for

their colony that set up a somewhat **democratic** government. This document was called the Mayflower Compact. All the healthy men of Plymouth signed the agreement.

Samoset surprised the Puritan colonists when he walked into their small settlement and greeted them by speaking English.

Women and children were expected to follow their husbands' and fathers' wishes.

The Pilgrims barely survived their first winter in Massachusetts. Many became sick with colds, fevers, and **scurvy,** the result of a poor diet. Nearly half the Pilgrims died.

In the spring, a Native American named Samoset was traveling near Plymouth. He walked into the village and shocked the settlers by saying, "Welcome, Englishmen." Samoset had learned English from traders he had met along the coast. Samoset soon brought the Wampanoag sachem Massasoit and a warrior called Tisquantum (called Squanto by the colonists) to meet the English.

Massasoit wanted friendship with the English. He signed a treaty with them that began nearly 50 years of peace. The English

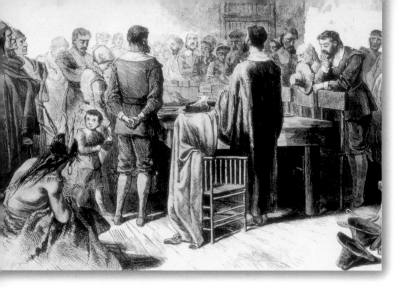

The first Thanksgiving was a way for the Pilgrims to show their gratitude to the Native Americans for showing them how to survive.

and the Native Americans swore to protect each other in case of attack.

In the autumn of 1621, the Pilgrims held a three-day Thanksgiving feast. Massasoit's people, who outnumbered the settlers, joined them. They most likely ate deer, game birds (ducks, geese, or wild turkey), corn, beans, and rye bread.

The Pilgrims' success encouraged more settlers to try Massachusetts. In 1630, a group of **Puritans** set sail to establish the Massachusetts Bay Colony. Puritans followed a "purer," stricter form of the Church of England. Their leader, John Winthrop, said, "We shall be as a city upon a hill. The eyes of all people are upon us."

The Puritans were prepared for hardships. Eleven ships sailed together, carrying 700 people, 240 head of cattle, 60 horses, and food. They brought tools for building and supplies for planting crops. The Puritans built the town of Boston, which became the capital of Massachusetts.

16

A WAMPANOAG NAMED TISQUANTUM TAUGHT THE PILGRIMS HOW TO SURVIVE in Massachusetts. Tisquantum, called Squanto by English colonists, grew up in the Wampanoag village of Patuxet. He met Europeans as they explored the coast near his village. In 1614, Captain Thomas Hunt's crew kidnapped 24 Native Americans, including Tisquantum. They were sold into slavery in Spain. Somehow, Tisquantum escaped and traveled to England.

He lived with an Englishman named John Slany and learned to speak English. In 1619, Slany arranged for Tisquantum to sail to Newfoundland, Canada. Arriving back in North America, Tisquantum headed south to his village. To his horror, he found Patuxet abandoned. Everyone had died in an epidemic, most likely smallpox or measles. Alone, Tisquantum joined Massasoit's Wampanoag people.

In 1621, Tisquantum agreed to help the Pilgrims. He taught them how to grow corn, fish, and hunt. He pointed out local herbs used for medicine. The Pilgrims would not have survived without his help.

Chapter THREE

The Bay Colony

One member of the Massachusetts Bay Colony, John Eliot, was extremely active in converting Native Americans to Christianity.

IN ENGLAND, THE PURITANS HAD BEEN punished for their faith. They came to Massachusetts for the freedom to follow their beliefs. However, they did not allow others that same freedom.

Puritans insisted that local native people become Christians. Native Americans who followed the Puritan religion were called Praying Indians. They lived in Christian villages separate from the rest of their people. Many Praying Indian towns, such as Nantucket, New Plymouth, and Natick, were located between Boston and tribal villages.

Puritans punished or drove away people who disagreed with church leaders. Roger Williams, Anne Hutchinson, and Mary Dyer were three colonists who suffered for their ideas. Williams, a Puritan minister, arrived in Boston in 1631. He believed that church and state should be separate. He was also against forcing Native people to become Christians. He even said that colonists should pay Native Americans for their land. The Puritans put up with Williams's ideas for five years. Then, they forced him to leave Massachusetts. In 1636, Williams founded Rhode Island on the idea of freedom of religion.

Anne Hutchinson's trial showed that the Puritans' government wasn't much different than the British government that had driven them out of England.

Hutchinson and Dyer had strange thoughts for women of their time. In Puritan society, women were expected to do what men told them. Hutchinson believed that God spoke directly to his chosen people and that God's word did not need to come through minis-

19

ters. She preached to others about her ideas. Hutchinson's ideas challenged the power of Puritan leaders. They tried her in court and kicked her out of the Puritan church. She was jailed and then forced to leave Massachusetts.

Mary Dyer's crime was becoming a Quaker. Quakers believed that people should only swear loyalty to God, not to kings or governors. Because the Puritan church was also the government, the

Mary Dyer was another person who left England to practice her religion freely, but when she became a Quaker, the Colony condemned her to death.

Puritans didn't like this idea. Being a Quaker became a crime in Massachusetts. Dyer was forced to leave the colony. She refused to stay away, so the Puritans hanged her on June 1, 1660.

By this time, nearly 40,000 English lived in Massachusetts. The colony had changed a great deal since the Pilgrims had first arrived—especially for the Native Americans. The English had taken over Wampanoag hunting grounds and farmland. Native people were forced to follow Puritan laws and religion.

At this time, the sachem of the Wampanoag was a man named Metacom. The English called him King Philip. Metacom believed the Puritans had killed his brother. He also hated the Puritans because they continued to take over Wampanoag lands. He looked for any excuse to fight the settlers.

In 1675, his excuse arrived. A Christian Native American named John Sassamon was killed. The Puritans hanged three Wampanoags for the crime. Metacom and his men attacked and burned several English villages, starting what became known as King Philip's War.

Other groups, including the Nipmuc and the Pocumtuck, joined the Wampanoag in their

Metacom, or King Philip, was the son of Massasoit, the Wampanoag sachem with whom the colonists had signed a peace treaty some 50 years earlier.

▶ Native Americans who did not join King Philip in his war against the settlers were regarded with suspicion on both sides. Sadly, the Puritans moved most of these peace-seeking people from their villages to islands in Boston Harbor to make sure they wouldn't join with Philip.

fight against the English. Fifty English villages were burned or damaged. Six hundred English and 3,000 Native Americans died. Another 500 Native Americans were sold into slavery, including Metacom's wife and son. He said, "My heart breaks . . . I am ready to die." In 1676, Metacom was shot through the heart and killed, ending King Philip's War. It was the worst fighting ever on Massachusetts soil.

By the war's end, very few Native Americans remained in the colony. They had almost all died or left Massachusetts to join other Native groups in places such as Canada and New York.

Brookfield was the first of many Massachusetts towns to be completely destroyed during King Philip's War.

Meanwhile, the English settlements were growing into bustling towns. Town life centered on the church, and everyone attended Sunday services.

This engraving by Paul Revere depicts Boston Harbor as a busy and important port even while the city was still new and growing.

Men worked as blacksmiths, shoemakers, barrel makers, potters, or millers. Women worked as tailors, shopkeepers, and innkeepers. They also took care of their families and homes. Towns with 50 households were required by law to support a school. Colonists wanted their children to be able to read the Bible.

Colonists traded with England for finished goods, such as glass, furniture, and cloth. In turn, the colonists sold whale oil, furs, timber, and rum. Some traders developed a profitable system. Boston merchants bought molasses from the West Indies to be turned into rum. They sold the rum to England. Money from the rum was used to pay for trips to Africa to buy or kidnap people, who were sent to the West Indies and sold as slaves. Enslaved people there worked the sugarcane fields that supplied

In the 1700s, Boston became a bustling center of trade for merchants from faraway lands and other New England towns.

molasses for making rum. Trade also brought slavery to Massachusetts. In 1708, the colony had about 550 slaves. Later in the 18th century, the number of enslaved people in Massachusetts grew to between 4,000 and 5,000.

In the 1750s, Massachusetts still belonged to Great Britain. At that time, the British and the French were arguing over the rich farmland and the fur trade in the Ohio River valley, far to the west of Massachusetts. The French and Indian War, which lasted from 1754 to 1763, settled the matter. In the end, Great Britain won all land east of the Mississippi River.

It might seem that the French and Indian War had nothing to do with Massachusetts. But the war had been very expensive for Great Britain. The British decided that the colonists should pay the costs of winning the war. They began putting high taxes on everyday items such as tea, coffee, and sugar. This set the colonies on the path to revolution.

SALEM, MASSACHUSETTS, WAS A DANGEROUS PLACE TO LIVE IN 1692. PEOPLE didn't dare do anything even slightly strange. If they did, they might be accused of witchcraft.

In January 1692, Tituba, an enslaved Caribbean woman, was taking care of 9-year-old Elizabeth Parris and 11-year-old Abigail Williams. Tituba told the girls about witchcraft. The girls started barking like dogs, shaking, and screaming. Other young girls began doing the same. Salem's doctor believed the girls were possessed by the devil.

Elizabeth and Abigail accused Tituba and two other women of casting spells on them. Tituba confessed, claiming that there were many witches in Salem. The people of Salem started suspecting everyone around them of witchcraft.

Over a few months, 100 people were tried as witches. Some of the accused witches were put to the "floating" test. They were tied hand and foot and tossed into a pond. If they floated, that proved they were a witch. Then they would be hanged. Sinking proved that they were innocent, but unfortunately they had already drowned.

Twenty people were put to death before the witchcraft trials ended. After some respected people were accused of witchcraft, other people began questioning the truth of the charges. In October 1692, the governor of Massachusetts stopped the Salem witch trials.

The Shot Heard 'Round the World

Interesting Fact

▶ According to the Quartering Act of 1765, the colonists were also expected to pay for the British soldiers' transportation expenses, the beer and cider they drank, and even the candles that lit their rooms at night.

THE BRITISH TAX LAWS ANGERED THE COLONISTS. Because the colonists did not send representatives to **Parliament** in England, they claimed it was "taxation without **representation.**"

The first of the new tax laws was the Sugar and Molasses Act of 1764. This law added costs to cloth, coffee, wine, and sugar. The Stamp Act came next, charging tax on all printed materials, even playing cards. The Quartering Act required the colonies to feed and house soldiers at their own expense. In many cases, soldiers lived in colonists' homes and ate with their families. The Townshend Acts of 1767 added taxes on glass, lead, paint, paper, and tea. By this time, the colonists had had enough.

Many British soldiers were quartered in Boston, and the people of Boston were very unhappy about it. On March 5, 1770, a boyish prank turned to killing. Some boys threw snowballs at a British soldier. Other British soldiers ran to help their friend, and Bostonians poured into the streets to support the boys. The soldiers shot into the crowd, killing five colonists. The first man shot was Crispus Attucks, a free African-American. Angry Bostonians called the event the Boston Massacre.

This engraving by Paul Revere of the Boston Massacre was spread throughout the colonies. It helped to further stir up the colonists' anger against the British.

Bostonians were also angry about the high taxes on tea. In 1773, some Bostonians saw a chance to protest the tax. One night, a group of men snuck onto three ships in Boston Harbor and dumped 342 cases of tea into the water. This event became known as the Boston Tea Party.

The Boston Tea Party on the night of December 16, 1773, is one of the most famous uprisings against British rule.

Colonists also protested the taxes by refusing to buy goods that were taxed. For example, many women stopped buying imported cloth, which was taxed. Instead, they began making their own cloth to use for their families' clothing.

By 1775, the people of Massachusetts had reached their breaking point. They formed a militia, or part-time army, called the Minutemen. The Minutemen were specially picked and trained. They claimed they were ready to fight the British on a "minute's" notice.

On a dark April night, a colonist named Paul Revere raced from Boston on horseback to tell the Minutemen that British troops were on the move. Fighting broke out in the nearby towns of Lexington and Concord on April 19, 1775. The start of this battle is called the "shot heard 'round the world." It changed history. The American Revolution had begun.

In June 1775, the Americans fought the British in a battle on Breed's Hill and Bunker Hill. British General William Howe led his troops into heavy musket fire. The Americans fought until they ran out of bullets. Then they withdrew. The British had won the battle, but 40 percent of the British soldiers who fought in it had been killed or wounded.

The British won many battles in the beginning of the war. But by early 1776, the war in Massachusetts changed. The Americans built a fort on a hill overlooking Boston Harbor. They aimed cannons at British ships and troops. Within two weeks, the British abandoned Massachusetts. The war continued for another seven years in the middle, southern, and Caribbean colonies before peace finally came in 1783.

When the first battle of the Revolutionary War broke out at now-famous Lexington Green, 77 Patriot Minutemen were there to bravely face their British enemies.

THOUGH OTHER WOMEN WORE UNIFORMS DURING THE AMERICAN Revolution, the story of Deborah Sampson is unusual. She so wanted to help in the fight for independence that she dressed as a man and fought in the Revolution. Sampson joined the army on May 20, 1782, using the name Robert Shurtleff.

Sampson was wounded in more than one battle. She was shot twice in the leg, and she was also cut with a sword. She cared for her own wounds to stop others from learning that she was a woman.

Finally, Sampson developed a fever and was sent to a hospital in Philadelphia, Pennsylvania. Her doctor quickly discovered that Shurtleff was really a woman. Sampson, still dressed as Robert Shurtleff, was given a letter to carry to General George Washington. The letter explained that Shurtleff was really Deborah Sampson. Washington gave Sampson an **honorable discharge,** and she returned to Massachusetts.

30

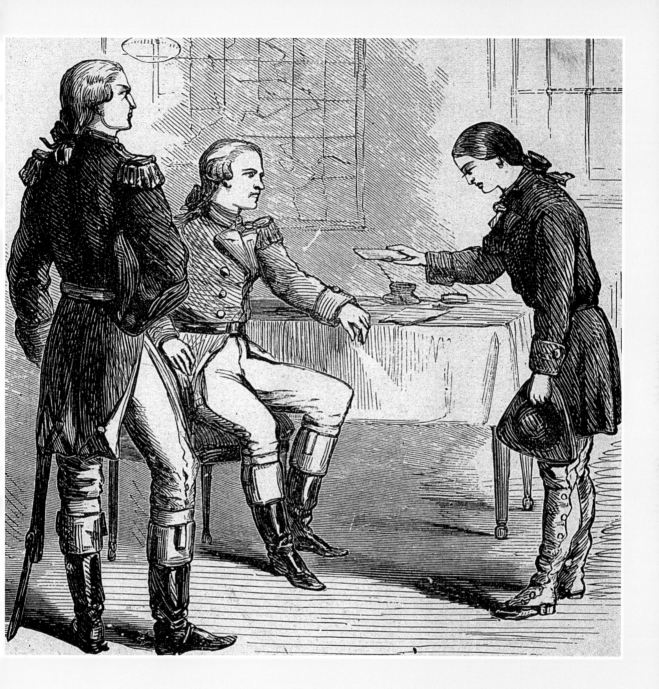

In 1792, the Massachusetts General Court gave Sampson money for her service in the army. The court said, "Deborah exhibited an extraordinary instance of female heroism." Twelve years later, Paul Revere sent a letter to the U.S. Congress about Sampson. She was awarded a U.S. Army **pension** of $4 per month.

Chapter FIVE

The Sixth State

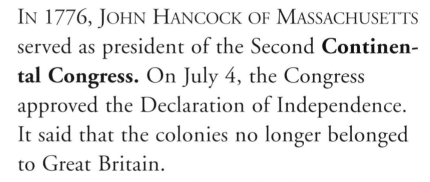

John Hancock was the first to sign the Declaration of Independence. His bold signature, as it appeared on that document, is well-recognized even today.

IN 1776, JOHN HANCOCK OF MASSACHUSETTS served as president of the Second **Continental Congress.** On July 4, the Congress approved the Declaration of Independence. It said that the colonies no longer belonged to Great Britain.

Hancock was the first person to sign the Declaration of Independence. He wrote his name very large because he wanted everyone to know he supported the break from England. John Adams, Samuel Adams, Elbridge Gerry, and Robert Paine also signed for Massachusetts.

In 1780, Massachusetts adopted a **constitution** to set up a state government. It is the oldest state

John Hancock was the first to sign the Declaration of Independence. His bold signature, as it appeared on that document, is well-recognized even today.

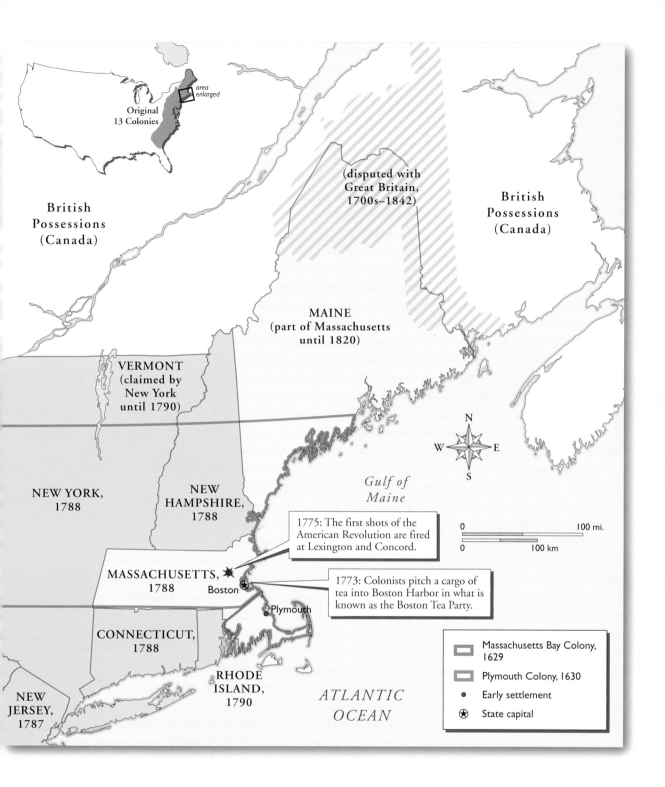

Original 13 Colonies

area enlarged

British Possessions (Canada)

British Possessions (Canada)

(disputed with Great Britain, 1700s–1842)

MAINE
(part of Massachusetts until 1820)

VERMONT
(claimed by New York until 1790)

NEW YORK,
1788

NEW HAMPSHIRE,
1788

Gulf of Maine

N
W   E
S

1775: The first shots of the American Revolution are fired at Lexington and Concord.

MASSACHUSETTS,
1788

Boston

1773: Colonists pitch a cargo of tea into Boston Harbor in what is known as the Boston Tea Party.

Plymouth

0   100 mi.
0   100 km

CONNECTICUT,
1788

RHODE ISLAND,
1790

ATLANTIC OCEAN

NEW JERSEY,
1787

	Massachusetts Bay Colony, 1629
	Plymouth Colony, 1630
●	Early settlement
✪	State capital

Massachusetts Colony before statehood

During Shays' Rebellion many farmers resorted to violence in protest of high taxes. Here, a mob seizes the Massachusetts Court House.

constitution still in use. Hancock became the state's first governor.

After the fighting ended in the Revolutionary War, states banded together under the **Articles of Confederation.** Under this agreement, the country had a very weak central government. The national government did not even have the power to raise money through taxes. Some people thought the nation needed a much stronger central government. But others worried that a strong central government would take power away from the individual states.

In 1786, Shays' Rebellion broke out in Massachusetts. The state government had enacted high taxes to pay for the war. Many poor farmers could not afford to pay these taxes. Some were in danger of losing their land. Mobs of people who owed money tried to close down the courts that were taking people's farms. Troops were sent in to stop them. The unrest of Shays' Rebellion left many people believing that a stronger national government was needed.

Representatives from the states got together and drew up the United States Constitution to replace the Articles of Confederation. On February 6, 1788, Massachusetts became the sixth state to approve the Constitution.

But before Massachusetts approved the Constitution, its representatives insisted that a list of personal rights be added. A few years later, it was. The **Bill of Rights** grants Americans many rights, including freedom of the press, of religion, and of speech. Americans owe Massachusetts thanks for many of the rights they enjoy.

Representatives gather in Philadelphia to create a new government and a stronger central democracy.

35

1498   John Cabot explores the Massachusetts coast.

1602   Bartholomew Gosnold names Cape Cod.

1620   English Separatists arrive at Plymouth aboard the *Mayflower*. The Mayflower Compact is signed.

1621   English colonists and local Native Americans hold the first Thanksgiving.

1630   English colonists establish the city of Boston.

1636   Roger Williams is forced out of Massachusetts for speaking against the Puritan church.

1675–1676   The Wampanoag and other Native Americans fight the English in King Philip's War. By its end, few native people remain in Massachusetts.

1692   The Salem witchcraft trials begin.

1754   France and Great Britain begin fighting the French and Indian War.

1764   The British pass the Sugar and Molasses Act, a tax on sugar, coffee, wine, and cloth.

1765   The British pass the Stamp Act, a tax on all printed materials.

1767   The British put a tax on tea and other goods.

1770   British soldiers kill five colonists in the Boston Massacre.

1773   Colonists pitch a cargo of tea into Boston Harbor in what is known as the Boston Tea Party.

1775   The first shots of the American Revolution are fired at Lexington and Concord.

1776   The Declaration of Independence is approved. John Hancock of Massachusetts is the first person to sign it.

1781   The Articles of Confederation becomes law for all states.

1788   The U.S. Constitution is approved. Massachusetts becomes the sixth state of the United States.

1791   The Bill of Rights is added to the U.S. Constitution.

Glossary TERMS

Articles of Confederation (AR-tih-kuhls uhv kuhn-FED-ur-ay-shun)
The Articles of Confederation was the first constitution for the United States. It was replaced in 1787 by the U.S. Constitution.

Bill of Rights (bil uhv rites)
The Bill of Rights is the first 10 amendments, or changes, to the U.S. Constitution. These amendments guarantee individual rights.

constitution (kon-stuh-TOO-shun)
A constitution is a written document that sets up a government. The U.S. Constitution came into effect in 1787.

Continental Congress (kon-tuh-NIHN-tuhl KONG-griss)
The Continental Congress was a meeting of colonists that served as the American government during the Revolutionary War. Each colony sent a number of representatives to the Congress.

democratic (dem-uh-KRAT-ik)
A democratic country is one where the government is chosen by the people. The colonists wanted a democratic government.

epidemics (ep-uh-DEM-iks)
Epidemics are major outbreaks of disease. Native Americans suffered through a number of epidemics after Europeans came to North America.

honorable discharge (ON-ur-ah-buhl DISS-charj)
An honorable discharge is a release from the army with a good reputation. General George Washington gave Deborah Sampson an honorable discharge.

Parliament (PAR-luh-muhnt)
Parliament is the lawmaking part of the British government. American colonists resented the taxes that were placed upon them by Parliament.

pension (PEN-shuhn)
A pension is money paid to a person after retirement. Very few women received a pension after the Revolutionary War.

Pilgrims (PIL-gruhms)
The English colonists who settled in Plymouth, Massachusetts, in 1620 were called Pilgrims. They were seeking religious freedom.

Puritans (PYOOR-uh-tuhns)
The Puritans were early American colonists who wanted a "purer" form of religion than was practiced in England. Today, the Puritans are more commonly called Pilgrims.

representation (rep-ri-zen-TAY-shuhn)
Representation is the right to have someone speak on behalf of a group of people. The colonists wanted representation in the British Parliament.

scurvy (SKUR-vee)
Scurvy is a deadly disease caused by not getting enough vitamin C. At the time of the Pilgrims, many people sailing on long voyages suffered from scurvy.

Separatists (SEP-uh-rah-tists)
Separatists were people who wanted to break away from the Church of England. They left Great Britain to settle in North America.

West Indies (WEST IN-deez)
The West Indies are islands that separate the Atlantic Ocean from the Caribbean Sea. Africans were sent to the West Indies and sold as slaves.

John Adams (1735–1826)

Continental Congress delegate, 1774–78; Declaration of Independence signer; diplomat to France, 1776–79; U.S. minister to the British court, c. 1785–88; U.S. vice-president, 1789–92; U.S. President, 1797–1801

Samuel Adams (1722–1803)

Massachusetts legislature member, 1765–74; Continental Congress delegate, 1774, 1775; Declaration of Independence signer; Articles of Confederation signer; Massachusetts governor, 1794–97, U.S. House of Representatives member, 1781

Francis Dana (1743–1811)

Continental Congress delegate, 1776–78; 1784–85; Articles of Confederation signer; secretary to John Adams in France; U.S. minister to Russia, 1780–83; Massachusetts supreme court associate justice, 1785–91; Massachusetts supreme court chief justice, 1791–1806

Elbridge Gerry (1744–1814)

Continental Congress delegate, 1776–81, 1783–85; Declaration of Independence signer; Articles of Confederation signer; Massachusetts governor, 1810, 1811; U.S. vice president, 1812–14

John Hancock (1737–1793)

Massachusetts state legislature, 1769–74; Continental Congress delegate, 1775–80, 1785, 1786; Continental Congress president, 1775–77; Declaration of Independence signer; Articles of Confederation signer; Massachusetts governor, 1780–85, 1787–1793

Samuel Holton (1738–1816)

Continental Congress delegate, 1778–80, 1783–85, 1787; Articles of Confederation signer; U.S. House of Representatives member 1793–95; justice of county probate court, 1796–1815

Rufus King (1755–1827)

Massachusetts state legislature, 1783–84; Continental Congress delegate, 1784–87; Constitutional Convention delegate, 1787; U.S. Constitution signer; 1788; U.S. Senator for Pennsylvania, 1789–96, 1813–25; U.S. Minister to Great Britain, 1796–1803, 1825–26

Robert Treat Paine (1731–1814)

Continental Congress delegate, 1774–78; Declaration of Independence signer; Massachusetts attorney general; Massachusetts supreme court justice, 1790–1804

Caleb Strong (1745–1819)

Constitutional Convention delegate, 1787; Massachusetts governor, 1800–1807, 1812–16; U.S. senator, 1789–96

For Further INFORMATION

Web Sites

Visit our homepage for lots of links about the Massachusetts colony:
http://www.childsworld.com/links.html

Note to Parents, Teachers, and Librarians:
We routinely verify our Web links to make sure they're safe,
active sites—so encourage your readers to check them out!

Books

Cox, Clinton. *Come All You Brave Soldiers: Blacks in the Revolutionary War.*
New York: Scholastic, 1999.

Furbee, Mary Rodd. *Outrageous Women of Colonial America.* New York: John
Wiley & Sons, 2001.

Hakim, Joy. *Making Thirteen Colonies.* New York: Oxford Press, 1999.

Places to Visit or Contact

Salem Office of Tourism and Cultural Affairs
To see historic homes, museums, and relics of the famed Salem witch trials
63 Wharf Street
Salem, MA 01970
877/725-3662

Plimoth Plantation
To visit a Wampanoag home and tour a replica of the Mayflower
137 Warren Avenue
Plymouth, MA 02362
508/746-1622

Index

Adams, John, 32
Adams, Samuel, 32
Algonquian tribes, 7
American Revolution, 28–29
animal life, 6
Articles of Confederation, 34
Attucks, Crispus, 27

Bill of Rights, 35
Boston, 16
Boston Massacre, 27
Boston Tea Party, 27
Breed's Hill, 29
Bunker Hill, 29

Cabot, John, 12
Concord, 28
Constitution of the United States, 35
Continental Congress, 32
Corte-Real, Miguel, 12–13

Declaration of Independence, 32
diseases, 10, 17
Dyer, Mary, 19, 20

France, 24
French and Indian War, 24
fur trade, 23, 24

Gerry, Elbridge, 32
Gosnold, Bartholomew, 13
government, 14–15, 20
grand sachem, 8
Great Britain, 11, 18, 23, 24,
    26–27, 29, 32

Hancock, John, 32
Howe, William, 29
Hunt, Thomas, 17
Hutchinson, Anne, 19–20

King Philip's War, 11, 21–22

Lexington, 28

Massachuset tribe, 8, 10
Massachusetts Bay Colony, 16
Massasoit, 11, 15–16
Mayflower Compact, 14–15
Metacom (Wampanoag sachem),
    11, 21, 22
Minutemen, 28
Mohican tribe, 8

Native Americans, 7–11, 15–16, 17,
    19, 21–22
Nipmuc tribe, 8

Paine, Robert, 32
Parris, Elizabeth, 25
Patuxet (Wampanoag village), 17
Pilgrims, 13, 14–16, 17
Plymouth colony, 14–15
Praying Indians, 18
Puritans, 11, 16, 18–21

Quakers, 20
Quartering Act, 26

Revere, Paul, 28, 31
Revolutionary War, 28-29, 34

sachems, 8, 11, 15, 21
Salem, 25
Samoset, 15
Sampson, Deborah, 30–31
Sassamon, John, 11, 21
Second Continental Congress, 32
Separatists, 13, 14
Shays' Rebellion, 34–35
Slany, John, 17
slavery, 11, 17, 23–24
Squanto. See Tisquantum.
Stamp Act, 26
state government, 34
Sugar and Molasses Act, 26

Tisquantum, 15, 17
Tituba (slave), 25
Townshend Act, 26

Vikings, 12

Wampanoag tribe, 8, 10, 11, 17,
    21–22
Wamsutta, 11
Washington, George, 30
wigwams, 9
Williams, Abigail, 25
Williams, Roger, 19
Winthrop, John, 16
witchcraft, 25

About the Author

BARBARA SOMERVILL IS THE AUTHOR OF MANY BOOKS FOR CHILDREN. She loves learning and sees every writing project as a chance to learn new information or gain a new understanding. Ms. Somervill grew up in New York State, but has also lived in Toronto, Canada; Canberra, Australia; California; and South Carolina. She currently lives with her husband in Simpsonville, South Carolina.